# SHIPPING AT CARDIFF

A typical example of Leslie Hansen's finely composed photography; the London-owned tramp steamer *Middlesex Trader* arriving at Cardiff, *c.* 1948.
(2090/2153)

# *Shipping at Cardiff*

## PHOTOGRAPHS FROM
## THE HANSEN COLLECTION
## 1920~1975

*David Jenkins*

UNIVERSITY OF WALES PRESS
NATIONAL MUSEUM OF WALES
2013

New edition, 2013

*www.uwp.co.uk*

*British Library Cataloguing-in-Publication Data*
A catalogue record for this book is available from the British Library.

ISBN 978-0-7083-2646-6

Published originally in 1993 with the financial support of The Baltic Exchange

Typeset by Hewer Text UK Ltd, Edinburgh
Printed by CPI Antony Rowe, Chippenham, Wiltshire

# Contents

# *Foreword*

I am delighted that the Baltic Exchange has been able to offer sponsorship to a book that illustrates the beauty of the ships with which our members have been associated in the past. It is also a personal pleasure and an honour to write the foreword for this book since I was born in Cardiff and have worked in shipping for forty years; the subject matter therefore has a special significance as many of the ships and owners are familiar to me.

The splendid Hansen archive provides a glimpse of times past for Cardiff. Today there are only a few shipowners remaining out of the 130 in business during the period when the port was most active, after the First World War.

This book is a beautifully illustrated record of the numerous ships once seen at the port. Although the Hansen Collection itself has been displayed (in part) at the Welsh Industrial and Maritime Museum, the publication of *Shipping at Cardiff* brings these marvellous photographs to the eyes of many more people and offers a descriptive narrative to accompany them. I offer warm congratulations to the author, David Jenkins, and I hope that the book is a great success.

PETER TUDBALL
CHAIRMAN, THE BALTIC EXCHANGE
1993

# Acknowledgements

The compilation of a photographic album such as this which comprises so many different ship photographs from the Hansen Collection has left me indebted to many individuals for their interest and assistance. My first thanks must go to the late Mrs Connie Hansen, Leslie Hansen's widow; without her approval of, and enthusiasm for, the publication of this album, it would have been almost impossible for me to proceed with the project. I am deeply indebted to her and her son Leslie, who welcomed me to their home in Mousehole, Cornwall, and told me so much about the Hansen family, and in particular about Leslie Hansen's career as a photographer. I also wish to thank all those who responded to my appeal published in the *South Wales Echo*, especially relatives and acquaintants of Leslie Hansen whose recollections have been most useful.

Many friends from Cardiff's shipping community have also been of great assistance. The principals of Cardiff's two remaining shipping firms – the late Mr D. C. Reid of Charles M. Willie & Co. (Shipping) Ltd. and the late Mr D. I. Williams of Idwal Williams & Co. Ltd. – supplied me with information on vessels once owned by their respective companies. The late Mr John O'Donovan proved to be a veritable fount of knowledge regarding the coasters and smaller sailing vessels illustrated in this album, whilst former Cardiff tug master the late Horace Patterson provided me with much detailed information on tugs and dredgers.

The former director of the National Maritime Museum, the late Dr Basil Greenhill, supplied me with useful information on certain sailing vessels and Mr Harold Appleyard, Mr J. J. Colledge and the late Mr Kevin O'Donoghue of the World Ship Society have also provided valuable assistance. I have relied heavily upon material already published on British and foreign shipping companies; the authors are acknowledged in the bibliography.

Amongst my colleagues at the Welsh Industrial and Maritime Museum, my greatest debt is to the museum's now retired Conservation Officer, Mr Don Taylor. Following the purchase of the Hansen Collection by the museum in 1979, it was he who undertook the formidable task of numbering and cataloguing all 4,565 negatives; had it not been for the characteristic thoroughness with which he undertook that job, this book could not have been contemplated. He was also of great help in preparing captions on the naval vessels. It was Mr Gordon Hayward, Senior Museum Assistant, who undertook the task of assembling batches of negatives to be sent for printing, and I am particularly grateful to Mr Kevin Thomas and his team in the National Museum's Photographic Department at the time for producing such fine prints for publication in this album. I also acknowledge the encouragement of Dr E. S. Owen-Jones, Keeper of the Welsh Industrial and

Maritime Museum and the co-operation of Mr Hywel Rees, Head of Publications at the National Museum of Wales. My thanks also to Ms Liz Powell and Mr Richard Houdmont at the University of Wales Press for their enthusiastic co-operation in the production of this volume. At the University of Wales Press, I am especially grateful to commissioning editor Sarah Lewis for suggesting the production of a second edition of *Shipping at Cardiff* and to Steven G. Goundrey and his colleagues at the Press for seeing the book through to its second appearance.

The publication of this volume has been made possible by most generous financial assistance granted by the Baltic Exchange, the world's foremost shipping market situated in the City of London. Many of the vessels illustrated in this album were owned by companies that were, or still are, represented 'on the Baltic'. But there is a more tangible link between Wales and the Baltic Exchange, as its chairman at the time of writing is Mr Peter Tudball, a native of Cardiff and the Baltic's first Welsh chairman. I am deeply grateful to Mr Tudball and his fellow directors for their interest and support, forthcoming at a time when they faced tremendous problems following the terrorist bomb attack on the Baltic Exchange in April 1992.

Finally, I wish to thank Mrs Sheila Charles for typing these acknowledgements and the introduction, and Mr Martin Rees for designing the map of Cardiff Docks.

*Unwaith eto, diolch yn fawr iawn i bawb.*

DAVID JENKINS
AMGUEDDFA CYMRU – NATIONAL MUSEUM WALES

# Introduction

One of the greatest treasures in the rich photographic archive of *Amgueddfa Cymru* – National Museum Wales is the Hansen Collection. The collection comprises 4,565 negatives (some two-thirds of which are glass) of ships at Cardiff, taken by members of the Hansen family between 1920 and 1975, providing a marvellous photographic record of shipping activity at the port during those years. In recent years numerous prints from negatives in this collection have appeared in publications by National Museum Wales, the World Ship Society and others, bringing to the attention of a wider audience the marvellous quality of the Hansens' shipping photography. It is hoped that this album, compiled in the centenary year of the foundation of Mr Hansen's photographic business, will further widen public interest in this collection, and bring to it the recognition it deserves as one of the finest of its kind in the British Isles.

The story behind the Hansen Collection begins not in Cardiff, nor even in Britain, but across the North Sea in Denmark. It was in this maritime nation's capital, Copenhagen, that Lars Peter Hansen was born in 1867. Like many of his fellow Danes, he chose the sea as a career, and whilst it is unclear in which capacity he served, or on board which ships, his voyaging eventually brought him to Cardiff. There were of course strong connections between the port of Cardiff and the Scandinavian countries. The great forests around the Baltic provided the booming coal industry of south Wales with pit wood, whilst many Scandinavians with expertise in shipping settled at Cardiff, most notably Harald Dahl (father of the author Roald Dahl) and Sir Sven Hansen. The little Lutheran church on the West Bute Dock not only provided a spiritual focus for the Scandinavian community in Cardiff, but was also a congenial place of recreation for visiting seamen from Denmark, Sweden and Norway.

Family tradition in the Hansen family rhaintains that Lars Peter had developed an interest in photography whilst he was still at sea, taking photographs of ships that he then sold to his fellow seamen. He eventually decided to settle in Cardiff in 1891, living at 4 North Church Street with his wife Rosa, a native of Newport. During the following years he would have had the chance to record shipping at Cardiff as the port rose to its commercial peak in 1913. In 1891, a total of nearly 7 million tons of coal was exported from the port; by 1913, this had risen to 10½ million tons. Unfortunately no negatives from this early period appear to have survived, though the present writer has had sight of photographs of vessels lost in the First World War that bear the Hansen imprint. Virtually the only shortcoming of the surviving Hansen negatives is that very few are precisely dated; the earliest negative in the present collection that can be dated approximately is of the French barque *Bonneveine*, which Dr Basil

Lars Peter Hansen, 1867–1947

Probably the earliest surviving Hansen negative is this view of the 2,617 gross ton French barque *Bonneveine* photographed by Lars Peter Hansen arriving at Cardiff in 1921. (827)

Greenhill records as having arrived at Cardiff with a cargo of grain from south Australia in 1921.

Lars Peter and Rosa Hansen had a family of eight children, three sons and five daughters. All three sons developed an interest in photography and Alfred, the eldest child, eventually established a photography business in the Cardiff suburb of Canton. The second son, Hermond, was associated with his father's business for a while, later moving to Barry. The third son, Leslie, was born on 23 December 1911 and in 1936 he married Constance (Connie) Smith; she was the daughter of a stevedore at Sharpness docks and had come to Cardiff to work in a confectionery shop in Caroline Street, in the city centre. Upon their wedding they took over the business of L. P. Hansen & Sons, established by Lars Peter in 1891, and acquired a studio and dark room at 3 Bute Place, near the main dock entrance. The vast majority of the earliest half-plate glass negatives in the Hansen Collection are from 1936/7, so it may be assumed that these date from the commencement of Leslie Hansen's business in partnership with his wife at that time.

Cardiff in 1936 was not the booming port it had been prior to the First World War. The increasing use of oil as a maritime fuel had led to the loss of many important

Leslie Hansen in his teens, photographed by his father.

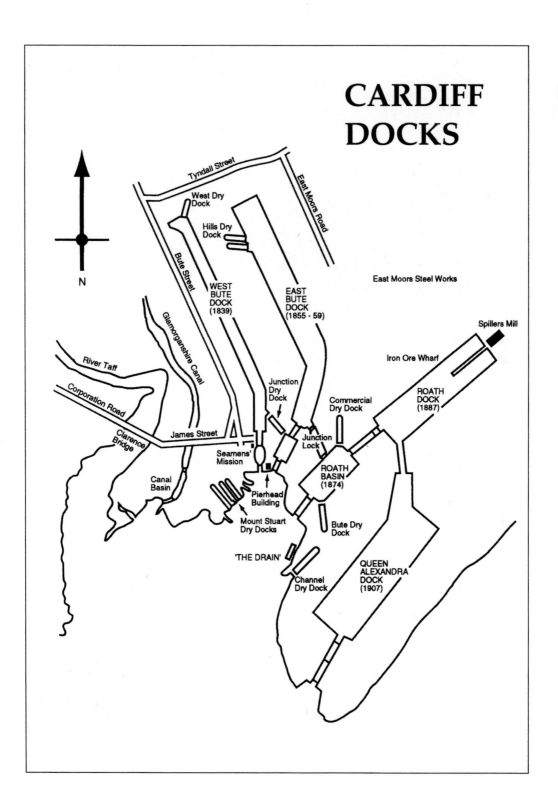

# CARDIFF DOCKS

REG. TONS                              BUILT                              GROSS TONS

LESLIE W. HANSEN, 3 BUTE PLACE, CARDIFF.

A photograph of the 2,908 gross ton steamer *Burdale* at Cardiff in 1947, showing the pattern of card mount used by Leslie Hansen for the sale of his prints.
(1437/1534)

European markets for south Wales steam coal, and increased exports of north American coal to south America had had an adverse effect on the once important River Plate trade. Nevertheless, coal exports from the port of Cardiff in the mid-1930s still averaged some 4½ million tons. Many ships also docked at Cardiff to take on bunkers, whilst others called to make use of the port's numerous ship-repair facilities. Some of the last commercial sailing vessels to use the port were also to be seen. There was therefore still plenty of shipping activity at Cardiff, and Mrs Connie Hansen recalls that her husband would be at either the Roath Basin lock or the Queen Alexandra lock at every daylight high tide unless he was otherwise engaged. This entailed carrying a cumbersome wooden camera and a large box full of half-plate glass negatives. The negatives would be taken back to the studio, developed and printed, and the prints were then mounted on cards giving details of the vessel portrayed, before being offered for sale to seamen and to the ship's owners.

With the outbreak of war in 1939, Leslie Hansen was not called up – instead he was retained as official photographer in the GWR's south Wales ports. Security restrictions during the war curtailed his general ship photography, with the result that there are no wartime negatives in the surviving Hansen Collection. The cessation of hostilities

Constance and Leslie Hansen photographed at a social event in the early 1950s.

brought about the end of restrictions and from 1946 until his retirement in 1975 Hansen's photography provides a marvellous picture of shipping in post-war Cardiff docks. The coal trade had gone into a further steep decline; exports in the later 1940s averaged some one million tons per annum, equal only to the figures of a century previously; in 1964 Cardiff ceased to be a coal-exporting port. Nevertheless, it is true to say that a greater variety of vessels could be seen in Cardiff docks from the late 1940s onwards, with the development of cold stores and oil termini attracting refrigerated vessels and oil tankers to a port once dominated by the deep sea tramps. Indeed, the demise of the traditional steam or motor-powered tramp and its replacement by more specialized vessels is another theme captured by Hansen's camera; he photographed the ore carriers of the late 1950s and the bulk carriers that brought cargoes of timber to be discharged on to spacious wharves where coal tips and sidings had once stood.

Photographing ships, however, was only one part of Leslie Hansen's business. He continued in his capacity as official photographer to the south Wales ports after their nationalization in 1947, in addition to which he also undertook architectural, advertising and legal photography. Amongst his numerous industrial commissions he photographed the building of the earliest stretches of the M4 in south Wales, the construction of the Royal Mint at Llantrisant and he was also retained by the Aberthaw cement works. He undertook much police work and specialized in the detailed photography required in complicated insurance cases. And as if this was not enough, most Saturdays saw him and his wife photographing weddings in and around Cardiff! As their son Leslie recalls, it was as much a way of life as a business to his parents, especially as it was Mrs Connie Hansen who handled all clerical matters.

Up until the early 1950s, Leslie Hansen would appear to have used glass negatives exclusively. As has been mentioned, almost all the pre-war photographs were taken on half-plate glass negatives, whilst quarter-plate glass negatives were used until about 1952. Thereafter Leslie Hansen went over to film, and all the negatives taken after the early 1950s are on 2¼" × 3¼" film. Whatever the type of negative used, however, the vast majority of the images recorded are superb. His composition was invariably faultless, with the vessel depicted always filling the frame. He was also an obvious master of darkroom technique as his negatives are all fine grain and their definition is always excellent.

Late in 1975 Leslie Hansen decided to retire from the business which he had handed over to his son, also named Leslie. Tragically, his retirement was to prove very short-lived, for he died suddenly on 22 April 1976. His son carried on the business (which by now was based at 95 Bute Street, between the Packet public house and the Midland Bank) for a few years but he found it increasingly difficult to run the enterprise profitably. Larger photographic firms with superior facilities and equipment had cornered much of the commercial market and in 1979, Leslie Hansen decided to sell up. The shipping negatives were then bought by the Welsh Industrial and Maritime Museum. The museum's conservation officer, Mr Don Taylor, undertook the massive task of re-numbering all the negatives; the numbers of the negatives reproduced in this album give the museum's number first, followed by Hansen's original number where this existed. The negatives

Leslie William Hansen, 1911–1976.

were then placed in individual negative bags and a 132-page catalogue was produced which is now available online at *www.amgueddfacymru.ac.uk/cy/rhagor/hansen*. The Hansen Collection is presently stored with the rest of the museum's photographic archive at the Collections Centre at Nantgarw, and can be consulted by prior appointment.

The tremendous historical value of the Hansen Collection cannot be overstated; it is on a par with the great collections of ship photography relating to other British ports such as the York Collection at Bristol. This album is intended as a tribute to Leslie Hansen and his father, who, through their work, have bequeathed to Wales such a marvellous record of shipping activity at the nation's premier port.

# ~ 1 ~

# Cardiff's Own

**1**

**1.** The brothers Philip and Thomas Morel had both moved to Cardiff from their native Jersey by 1862; by 1888 they had built up a fleet of twenty-three steamers. The steamer *Nolisement* dated from a later period in the firm's history, having been built at Newcastle in 1928. This 5,084 gross ton vessel survived the Second World War and was eventually cut up at Split in Yugoslavia early in 1966.
(2809/2832)

**2**

**3**

**2.** Morels were amongst the first Cardiff owners to acquire motor vessels, and in 1936–7 they took delivery of two Doxford 'Economy' motor tramps. The second of these was the 4,998 gross ton *Forest*, seen here in the Queen Alexandra Dock, *c.* 1948. Twice bombed during the Second World War, she was still trading under the Cypriot flag in the late 1960s.
(2425/2474)

**3.** John Cory was born in Padstow where he was already the owner of a number of sailing vessels before deciding to move to Cardiff in 1872. By 1900 his sons were operating a fleet of twenty-three steamers. The steamer *Coryton* pictured here was a 4,553 gross ton vessel built at West Hartlepool in 1928; she is seen here in the Roath Dock, *c.* 1936. She was named after the Cory family home, which by today has given the name Coryton to a suburb in north Cardiff.
(221/423)

**4.** One of the last steamships owned at Cardiff was the handsome *Ramillies*, owned by John Cory & Sons from 1955 until 1966. Built at West Hartlepool in 1951 for London-Greek shipowners, she was an oil-fired steamer of 5,890 gross tons. She is seen here discharging iron ore at the East Moors terminal in the Roath Dock, *c.* 1964.
(4236/1R)

**5**

**6**

**5.** Evan Thomas, Radcliffe & Co. was founded in 1881 when Captain Evan Thomas of Aber-porth, Ceredigion, went into partnership with the young Merthyr-born clerk, Henry Radcliffe. Their venture prospered; on the eve of the First World War, the firm controlled twenty-eight vessels, Cardiff's largest fleet. The 4,680 gross ton *Peterston* was built at Sunderland in 1925 and served Radcliffe's until 1948, when she was sold; after a number of changes in ownership she was broken up at Antwerp in 1959. She is seen here in the Queen Alexandra Dock, *c.* 1947.
(1021/1122)

**6.** Many Radcliffe ships bore Welsh place-names which had the prefix 'Llan-', meaning church. The 5,055 gross ton *Llanberis* was named after the village at the foot of Snowdon, and was the third vessel in the Radcliffe fleet to bear this name. Built at Wallsend in 1928, she was sold to Greek owners in 1950. She is seen here discharging a cargo of sawn timber in the Queen Alexandra Dock, *c.* 1948.
(1596/1687)

**7.** The Radcliffe company was taken over by the Cardiff fuel factors Evans & Reid in 1947, and the ships were given new liveries and fleur-de-lys funnel markings in place of the 'Cardiff British India Line' black funnel and two white bands visible in the two previous photographs. The Sunderland-built *Llandaff* of 1937, a 4,826 gross ton steamer, is seen here arriving at Cardiff in the new colours, *c.* 1950. Sold to German owners in 1951, she was eventually stranded at Esbjerg in 1959 and broken up at Ghent later that year. The author's great-uncle, Captain John Rees Jenkins of Aber-porth, Ceredigion was the first master of this vessel when she joined the Radcliffe fleet in 1937.
(2933/2954)

8

9

**8.** Evans & Reid had been in shipping prior to their takeover of Radcliffe's in 1947. In 1931 Barclay's Bank entrusted the firm with the management of a number of steamers owned by former Cardiff shipowners on whom the bank had foreclosed. One of these was the 4,107 gross ton *Nailsea Moor*, formerly owned by Williams & Mordey of Cardiff as their *David Lloyd George*. Built at Stockton-on-Tees in 1917, she is seen here at Cardiff, *c.* 1936.
(95/189)

**9.** A tranquil scene is recorded in this view of the *Porthrepta* approaching the Queen Alexandra lock on 8 December 1947. She was owned by Care Lines, established at Cardiff in 1920 by Richard Penberthy Care. This 643 gross ton coaster was built at Glasgow in 1922. Care Lines were much involved in trade to the Channel Islands.
(1826/1906)

**10.** Although it was not until the late 1950s that P. & A. Campbell moved their head office from Bristol to Cardiff, most Cardiffians tended to regard the 'White Funnel' fleet as much their own as did the Bristolians! No summer was complete without a trip to Minehead or Ilfracombe on one of their paddle steamers. The *Glen Usk* was built at Troon in 1914 and her decks were crowded with trippers as she left Cardiff in this 1948 view. Laid up in the early 1960s, she was broken up at Passage West near Cork in 1963.
(2004/2072)

11

12

**11.** The *Cardiff Queen* was one of two similar paddle steamers ordered by P. & A. Campbell after the Second World War. Built at Govan in 1947, this 765 gross ton vessel was a little smaller than her sister *Bristol Queen*, built at Bristol in 1946. In this 1962 view, the *Cardiff Queen* is seen getting under way from the landing stages at the Pierhead. Withdrawn from service in 1966, she was eventually cut up at Newport in 1968.
(3354)

**12.** An unusual view of the *Bristol Queen* with the *Cardiff Queen* behind her; both vessels were undergoing pre-season repairs in the Bute Dry-dock in March 1962. Just to the right of the *Bristol Queen*'s foremast can be seen the bow of Reardon Smith's *Bradford City*, which is moored in the Roath Basin.
(3360)

**13.** The 5,222 gross ton steamer *Hadleigh* proceeding up 'the Drain' towards the Roath Basin lock, *c.* 1936. This vessel was built on the Tees in 1930 to the order of W. J. Tatem & Co. of Cardiff. Tatem was a native of Appledore who set up his own shipping venture in 1897, aged only twenty-nine. He built up a highly successful company and was one of the few Cardiff owners still paying dividends during the difficult inter-war years. The *Hadleigh* met her end during the Second World War, torpedoed and sunk by the German submarine *U-77* on 16 March 1943.
(315/540)

14

**14.** W. J. Tatem was elevated to the peerage in 1918, taking the title Lord Glanely. This 5,640 gross ton steamer was named after him upon its completion at Sunderland in 1947, but Tatem never saw the vessel as he lost his life during a bombing raid on Weston-super-Mare in 1942. The *Lord Glanely*, seen here at Cardiff in 1948, was sold to Pakistani owners in 1960 and broken up at Gadani Beach in 1973. (2508/2550)

**15.** The *J. Duncan* was owned by J. T. Duncan & Co. of Cardiff. Never a large firm, they operated a number of small steamers in the trades to the Bay of Biscay and on charter to the Admiralty as fleet colliers. This 1,832 gross ton vessel was built at Dublin in 1914 and traded until 1956 when she was sold for breaking up at Milford Haven. (799/H1078)

**16.** A fine study of the 3,660 gross ton steamer *Amicus* arriving at Cardiff, *c.* 1936. She was built on the Tyne in 1925 for W. H. Seager's Tempus Shipping Co. Ltd., Cardiff. Seager's roots were in Minehead and Ilfracombe and he established himself as a chandler at Cardiff in 1892, later entering into shipowning in 1904. The *Amicus* was lost on 19 December 1940 when she was torpedoed by an Italian submarine off the coast of Co. Mayo, Ireland. (228/430)

15

16

17

18

**17.** One of the last vessels owned by W. H. Seager & Co. was the 7,442 gross ton steamer *Beatus*, built in British Columbia, Canada in 1942 as the standard 'Fort' type wartime vessel, *Fort Tremblant*. Seen here at Cardiff in 1952, she was sold to J. A. Billmeir of London in 1955 and broken up at Hong Kong in 1963. Seagers ceased trading as shipowners in that same year.
(3223/3215)

**18.** The Reardon Smith Line was without doubt Cardiff's best-known shipping firm and was far and away the port's largest shipping enterprise during the inter-war years. Founded in 1905 by Captain William Reardon Smith, almost all the company's ships bore names with the 'City' suffix. The *Prince Rupert City* was a 4,749 gross ton steamer built at West Hartlepool in 1929; she is seen here arriving at Cardiff, *c.* 1937. On 2 June 1941 she was bombed and sunk by German aircraft north-east of Cape Wrath, with the loss of four crew members.
(138/264)

**19.** The Reardon Smith Line acquired motor vessels as early as 1928, though this example, the 4,928 gross ton *Devon City* was built for the firm at Haverton Hill in 1933. The firm certainly had value for money from her, for she was owned by Reardon Smith for twenty-five years before she was sold to Liberian owners in 1958! She was eventually wrecked off the mouth of the Orange River, South Africa, on 28 August 1967.
(2896/2914)

**19**

**20.** During the late 1960s, Reardon Smith and Upper Clyde Shipbuilders co-operated to produce a design for a 26,000 deadweight ton bulk carrier. The first of these vessels was built in 1970 and seven were built for Reardon Smith in addition to numerous others ordered for shipping firms world-wide. One of these 'Cardiff class' bulk carriers was the *Tacoma City* of 1972, seen here discharging timber at Cardiff in 1974. Ten years later, in October 1984, she became the last Reardon Smith vessel to visit Cardiff before the firm ceased trading in May 1985.
(4419/2T)

**21.** Cardiff's well-known Abbey Line was founded by marine engineer Frederick Jones in 1907. The 2,467 gross ton *Singleton Abbey* was built at Stockton-on-Tees in 1915 and she is seen here in the Roath Dock in 1936 with a deck cargo of timber from Russia. Note the considerable list to port that has developed on the homeward voyage. The *Singleton Abbey* was sold to other Cardiff owners in 1936 and sank after striking a mine in the English Channel in December 1941.
(74/136)

**22.** The Graig Shipping Co. Ltd. was founded in 1919 by Idwal Williams and is today one of Cardiff's two surviving shipping firms. The *Graig*, built at Port Glasgow in 1924, was the second vessel in the fleet to carry that name, which is Welsh for 'rock'. She was wrecked on the coast of Nova Scotia on 4 May 1940.
(98/212)

**23**

**24**

**23.** The *Graigddu*, seen here at Cardiff in 1948, was built at Sunderland in 1941 as the *Empire Mariott*. This 5,970 gross ton steamer was managed by Graig from 1944 until 1946; the company then bought her and gave her her new name, meaning 'black rock'. Sold to an Indian shipping firm in 1952, she was broken up at Bombay in 1969.
(2318/2369)

**24.** Cardiff's other surviving shipping firm is Charles M. Willie & Co. (Shipping) Ltd., formed in 1913. The company did not own their ships until 1929 when the 1,774 gross ton *Willodale*, built at Sunderland in 1909, was acquired. This photograph of her was taken as she left Bordeaux with a cargo of pit wood, *c.* 1936. Whilst this photograph may not have been taken by Hansen, it appears in the Hansen Collection, hence its inclusion in this book. The *Willodale* was lost off the estuary of the Gironde on 4 April 1947.
(4556/12W)

**25.** The 1,241 gross ton steamer *Empire Connell* was built at Sunderland in 1909 for Norwegian owners. Seized as a war prize during the Second World War, she was managed by Charles M. Willie & Co. from 1945 until 1947. Willie's main shipping activity today is the operation of regular liner services from UK ports to Spain and Portugal and the Baltic States of Estonia, Latvia and Lithuania.
(1112/1213)

26

**26.** The Claymore Shipping Co. Ltd. was established in 1919 by Charles Leigh Clay, father of the famous Glamorganshire off-spin bowler, J. C. Clay. In 1947 the company acquired the Liberty ship *Samdonard*, which they re-named *Daybeam*. Seen here in the Queen Alexandra Dock in 1950, her blue funnel with two yellow bands reflected the tie colours of the Glamorganshire Cricket Club. The *Daybeam* was sold to Panamanian owners in 1952 and was eventually cut up at Kaohsiung, Taiwan, in 1968.
(2999/3016)

**27.** The South American Saint Line had its origins in two separate companies both established in 1926. They were amalgamated to form the B. & S. Shipping Co. Ltd. in 1933 under the management of Richard Street. Street's ambition was to establish a regular cargo line to the River Plate, and a number of vessels were acquired in the late 1930s. One of these was the 4,312 gross ton *St Rosario*, built at Sunderland in 1937 and seen here at Cardiff in October 1947. Sold to Swedish owners in 1952, she was cut up in 1969.
(1738/1822)

**28.** After the Second World War, Richard Street ordered two new cargo liners to reinstate the service to South America. The first of these was the *St Essylt*, a 6,855 gross ton motor vessel, completed at Sunderland in 1948. These vessels were of revolutionary design and very modern appearance, and were considered to be the finest cargo vessels of their size in the British merchant fleet. Two further vessels of similar design were acquired in 1954 and 1961, but Richard Street's sudden death in that year led to the premature demise of the venture.
(2548/2587)

**29**

**30**

**29.** The 1,744 gross ton steamer *Ottinge* was built on the Tyne in 1918, and was acquired by Constants (South Wales) Ltd. in 1929. The Constant family were natives of Gravesend who transferred their head office from London to Cardiff in 1929. Most of their vessels were named after rural villages in Kent. In this 1936 view, the *Ottinge* is seen just off Cardiff's Pierhead, with the Mountstuart Dry-docks in the background.
(463)

**30.** It was in 1936 that John Lovering established the company of Lovering & Sons to acquire the Dutch-built motor coaster *Calyx*. He later acquired further efficient Dutch motor coasters such as the 353 gross ton *Cornel*, built at Westerbroek in 1938. She is seen here arriving at Cardiff in 1949.
(2818/2840)

**31.** Another Dutch-built coaster owned by Lovering & Sons was the 528 gross ton *Petertown*, built for London owners in 1938 and bought by Loverings in 1951. Seen here in the East Bute Dock in 1956, she was sold to Italian owners in 1959, the year in which Loverings ceased trading as shipowners.
(4204/14P)

**32.** The Hindlea Shipping Co. Ltd. was established in 1949 by R. D. Lean and J. L. Hindmarsh and in 1952 they bought the 402 gross ton motor coaster *Fennel* from Lovering & Sons. She was renamed *Hindlea* by her new owners. On 27 October 1959 she was blown ashore and totally wrecked near Moelfre, Anglesey, in a north-easterly gale similar to that which had wrecked the *Royal Charter* a century earlier. Coxswain Richard Evans of the Moelfre lifeboat was awarded his first RNLI gold medal for his rescue of the crew of the *Hindlea* on that terrible night.
(3891/32H)

**33.** The Cravos family were natives of Trieste where they owned a number of sailing vessels. They later moved to Cardiff, becoming shipowners at the port in 1914. The 4,576 gross ton steamer *Ampleforth* was built at Stockton-on-Tees in 1929 as *Glofield* for Humphries & Co. of Cardiff and was bought by Cravos in 1932. Seen here arriving at Cardiff, *c.* 1936, she was torpedoed and sunk in the north Atlantic on 18 August 1940.
(30/31)

**34.** The *South Wales* was a 5,619 gross ton steamer built at Sunderland in 1929 for Gibbs & Co. of Cardiff. The company had been founded in 1906, but moved its offices to Newport in 1950. They later went on to establish Welsh Ore Carriers in association with London & Overseas Freighters Ltd. of London. The *South Wales* was wrecked in the Belle Isle Strait off Newfoundland on 26 September 1941. Gibbs & Co. ceased trading as shipowners in 1989.
(78A/140)

**35.** The Chellew Steam Navigation Co. Ltd. had its origins in Truro in 1888 when R. B. Chellew bought his first steamship. The firm was taken over by Frank Shearman of Cardiff in 1920, and he maintained the practice of naming the firm's vessels after Cornish place-names starting with the prefix 'Pen-'. The 4,174 gross ton *Pendeen* was built for Chellew's at West Hartlepool in 1923 and is seen here in the Queen Alexandra Dock, *c.* 1948.
(990/1092)

**36.** A fine study of the 4,574 gross ton steamer *Grelrosa*, built at Newcastle in 1914, arriving at Cardiff with a cargo of pit wood, *c.* 1936. This vessel was operated by Walter Gould, whose cousin, James C. Gould, built up a massive fleet during the boom following the First World War, only to crash to failure in 1925. Walter Gould's shipping company survived until 1960.
(236/450)

# ~ 2 ~

# Coasters and Colliers

**37.** The 487 gross ton steam coaster *Ardri* was built at Glasgow in 1892 as *Coral* for Wm. Robertson's Gem Line. She was acquired by the well-known Amlwch-based shipbuilders and owners, William Thomas & Sons, in 1923 and was employed by them chiefly in the Irish Sea tramping trades. She is seen here arriving at Cardiff, *c.* 1935, not long before she foundered off Bardsey on 22 January 1936, whilst bound from London to Glasgow with a cargo of cement.
(503/H774)

**38**

**39**

**38.** The 2,473 gross ton steam collier *Sarastone* about to enter Barry Docks, *c.* 1936. Built at Burntisland, Fife, in 1929, this vessel was owned by Stone & Rolfe of Llanelli. On 22 December 1940 this vessel succeeded in fighting off an attack by the Italian submarine *Moncenigo*, but she was eventually bombed and sunk by German aircraft just after leaving the Spanish port of Huelva on 29 October 1941. (55/57)

**39.** The 965 gross ton steam coaster *Afon Morlais* approaching Cardiff with a deck cargo of timber, *c.* 1949. This vessel was built at Bowling in 1944 as *Empire Marksman* and was sold to William Coombs & Sons Ltd. of Llanelli in 1948 who re-named her in line with their practice of naming their ships after Welsh rivers. Sold to John S. Monks of Liverpool in 1956, she was eventually cut up at Dublin in 1958. (3414/40A)

**40.** The Harries brothers were natives of Fishguard who established themselves as shipowners at Swansea in 1888. In 1946 their company acquired the 2,066 gross ton steam coaster *Empire Peggotty*, built at Grangemouth in 1944 and she was renamed *Glanowen*. She is pictured here arriving at Cardiff, *c.* 1948. Sold to Liberian owners in 1965, she foundered in the estuary of the River Weser, northern Germany, on 12 March 1967. (1116/1218)

**41.** Probably the oldest vessel photographed by Hansen was this venerable 146 gross ton coaster, *Iron Duke*. Built at Glasgow in 1857, she started life as a paddletug in the fleet of the Cardiff Towing Company; she was later bought by J. B. Brain of Bristol who had her converted into a cargo vessel with screw propulsion. At the time this view was taken, *c.* 1936, she was owned by A. J. Smith & Co., Bristol who owned a number of small coasters engaged in the coal trade in the Bristol Channel. She is towing a Severn trow, the traditional sailing barge of the Severn Estuary. She was lost when she struck a mine near the Breaksea light vessel in May 1941.
(788/H1065)

**42.** In direct contrast to the aged *Iron Duke* is this 454 gross ton motor coaster *Castle Combe*, owned by Ald Shipping, also of Bristol. Built at Bristol in 1936, she was the first of a number of similar motor vessels built for this firm. The *Castle Combe* was one of the last vessels to load anthracite at Saundersfoot in Pembrokeshire in the 1930s. Ald Shipping ceased trading in 1960.
(550/H823)

**43.** The 570 gross ton steam coaster *Lakewood* was owned by the splendidly named Onesimus Dorey & Sons of St Peter Port, Guernsey. Built at Aberdeen in 1919, she is seen here taking on bunkers at the bottom of the East Bute Dock, *c.* 1948. Dorey's vessels were regular visitors to ports in south Wales, loading cargoes of coal for Guernsey's gasworks and anthracite to warm the island's many glasshouses.
(1671/1759)

42

43

**44.** Richard Hughes was born at Gronant in Flintshire in 1858 and in 1884 he commenced business as a shipowner in Liverpool, acquiring the steam coaster *Primrose*. Most of his subsequent vessels were given names that incorporated the word 'rose', and his firm came to be known generally as the 'Rose Line' The 739 gross ton *Moss Rose* was built at Hardinxveld in the Netherlands in 1930; she is pictured here sailing up 'the Drain', *c.* 1936. Sold to Greek shipowners in 1960, she was later fitted with a diesel engine before she was eventually cut up at Perama in Greece in 1973.
(359/657)

**45.** The steam coaster *Bankville*, built at Troon in 1904, was owned by the well-known Liverpool coaster owners, John S. Monks & Co. Ltd. This 339 gross ton vessel provides an excellent illustration of the most basic type of British-built steam coaster, with her mast and derrick serving one large hatch, engines postioned aft, and an open bridge. Many of these little coasters had remarkably long careers and the *Bankville* plied the coasts of Britain for over fifty years before she was cut up at Dublin in 1957.
(517/H791)

**46.** James Fisher & Sons of Barrow was established in 1847 and they operated a substantial fleet of sailing vessels before they acquired their first steamer in 1883. The *Pool Fisher* was a steam coaster of 605 gross tons, built at Barnstaple in 1921; with her long raised quarter-deck and bridge amidships, she is typical of the larger type of British steam coaster. She is pictured here sailing up 'the Drain' on a murky day, *c.* 1947. Fishers remain in business as shipowners today, managing a varied fleet that comprises a number of vessels designed for the carriage of nuclear fuel and waste.
(2402/2452)

45

46

47

48

**47.** A regular visitor to Cardiff for many years was the 1,061 gross ton steamer *Beauty*. Built at Troon in 1924, she was one of the vessels that maintained the weekly cargo service operated by William Sloan & Co. Ltd. of Glasgow from the Clyde to Swansea, Cardiff and Bristol. She was originally built with accomodation for passengers, but this was removed in 1932. Seen here sailing up 'the Drain' to the warehouse on the East Bute basin, *c*. 1948, she was eventually scrapped at Antwerp in May 1959. (2556/2594)

**48.** One of the best-known of all British coasting shipowners was William Robertson of Glasgow, whose company was known as the 'Gem Line' as a result of his naming his vessels after precious and semi-precious stones. His first steam coaster was the *Agate* of 1878; only eighteen years later the 678 gross ton *Pearl* (shown here) was built to his order at Glasgow. Robertsons remained in business as independent shipowners until 1970 when they were taken over by the Powell Duffryn subsidiary Stephenson Clarke of London. (2346/2396)

**49.** John Stewart established a business as a ship sale and purchase broker at Glasgow in 1899, but he decided to move into shipowning in the 1920s, acquiring his first steam coaster in 1923. The 823 gross ton *Yewtree* was built to his order at Bowling in 1928 and is seen here in the Roath Basin, *c*. 1948. The company's vessels were nicknamed the 'Yew-boats', an amusing pun on the name generally given to German submarines in both world wars. (2575/2609)

**50.** A large coasting fleet whose vessels were to be seen regularly at Cardiff was that owned by John Kelly Ltd. of Belfast. Founded by Samuel Kelly in the 1840s, the company relied on sailing vessels until they acquired their first steamer in 1890. The 581 gross ton steam coaster *Carrickmore* was built at Aberdeen in 1925 and she is seen here approaching the Queen Alexandra lock, *c.* 1936. In 1948, the company was acquired jointly by William Cory & Sons and Powell Duffryn, though it was only late in 1990 that the four remaining Kelly vessels were fully integrated into the Powell Duffryn fleet.
(553/H825)

**51.** Snow is visible on the ground in Penarth as the 347 gross ton steam coaster *Thorn* manoeuvres off the entrance to the Queen Alexandra Dock, *c.* 1947. Built at Bowling in 1934, she was owned by Joseph Fisher of Newry. This company was established with a fleet of sailing vessels in 1852, and they acquired their first steamer in 1889. The Fisher company was eventually taken over by the Belfast fuel factors, Cawoods, in 1966.
(1388/1487)

**52.** A charming view of the 979 gross ton steam coaster *Holderness* sailing from the Queen Alexandra lock, Cardiff, *c.* 1957. She was built at Wivenhoe in 1920 as *Maindy Tower* for Cardiff's Maindy Shipping Co. Ltd., and was eventually acquired by the Holderness Steamship Co. Ltd. of Hull in 1955. She had served her new owners for four years only when she went aground at Blyth in March 1959 and became a constructive total loss.
(3906/39H)

**53.** The 2,831 gross ton steam collier *Lambtonian* was completed at Sunderland in 1942 for the Tanfield Steamship Co. Ltd. of Newcastle, the shipping arm of the Lambton and Hetton Collieries Ltd. During the war she acted as commodore ship on 111 East Coast convoys, and she was also in the first merchant convoy to France on D-Day. She was sold to Stephenson Clarke of London in 1952 and was broken up at Dunston in 1960. In this view, she is seen arriving at Cardiff with a deck cargo of pit wood, *c.* 1948. (1702/1788)

**54.** The 567 gross ton steam coaster *Moray Firth* approaching the Roath Basin lock, *c.* 1948. She was owned by G. T. Gillie & Blair of Newcastle, a firm originally established by G. T. Gillie in 1911. The *Moray Firth* was sold to the Aberdeen Coal & Shipping Co. Ltd. in 1959, and was eventually broken up at Dunston in March 1972. G. T. Gillie & Blair still operate a fleet of owned and managed coasters from Newcastle today. (2400/2450)

**55.** Proudly claiming itself to be 'the world's largest coastwise liner fleet', Coast Lines was the name given in 1917 to an agglomeration of three of Britain's foremost coastal liner firms formed in 1913. Between 1917 and its eventual demise when taken over by P. & O. in 1970, Coast Lines came to dominate Britain's coastal liner trade with a voracious policy of acquiring other firms and their services. The *British Coast*, built at Leith in 1934, was typical of the motor vessels built for Coast Lines in the inter-war years, and the 889 gross ton vessel had accomodation for twelve passengers. Seen here sailing up 'the Drain' to the firm's warehouse in the East Bute Dock, *c.* 1948, the *British Coast* was sold in 1964. (1386/1485)

**56.** The 1,128 gross ton coasting tanker *Daxhound* was built at Hamburg in 1931 and eight years later was acquired by Hadley Shipping of London, established in 1926. She usually operated on time charter to the Petroleum Board, and is seen here approaching the East Bute Basin, *c.* 1948. She was sold back to German owners in 1951. Hadley Shipping is still in existence and the company currently operates a number of bulk carriers of various sizes.
(2058/2123)

**57.** F. T. Everard & Sons commenced business as shipowners in 1892 with the purchase of a Thames sailing barge. The firm subsequently expanded to become one of the foremost owners of coastal cargo vessels and tankers in Britain. The 798 gross ton *Allegrity* was built at Grangemouth in 1945 as the *Empire Tavistock*, one of twenty-three coastal tankers of a type known as the 'Cadet' class. Acquired by Everards in 1951, she is seen here approaching the Queen Alexandra lock, *c.* 1953. The *Allegrity* went aground on St Anthony Head, Cornwall in December 1961; she was refloated, but capsized shortly afterwards on 22 December 1961.
(3216/3209)

# ~ 3 ~

# *Tramps, Tankers and Liners*

**58.** One of Britain's best-known tramping firms was the Hain Steamship Co. Ltd. which had its origins in the purchase by Edward Hain of St Ives, Cornwall, in 1878, of the steamer *Trewidden*. Taken over by P. & O. in 1917, the firm continued to be run as a largely independent entity until the early 1970s. The 5,605 gross ton *Tremorvah* was built at Port Glasgow in 1954, and the distinctive 'H' funnel marking of the firm can be discerned in this view taken *c.* 1959. Sold to Greek owners in 1968, this handsome motor vessel was broken up at Hong Kong in 1978.
(4468/36T)

59

60

**59.** The 4,093 gross ton steamer *Dartford*, built at Middlesbrough in 1930, arriving at Cardiff, *c.* 1936. This vessel was owned by the London-based company of Watts, Watts & Co. which had its origins in a shipping agency established at Blyth in 1851. All their vessels were named after London suburbs; the *Dartford* had two identical sisters named *Deptford* and *Dulwich*. The *Dartford* was torpedoed and sunk in the north Atlantic on 12 June 1942. Watts, Watts & Co. were taken over by the Liverpool-based Bibby Line in 1968.
(161/319)

**60.** Turnbull, Scott & Co. Ltd. had its origins in Whitby, where the Turnbull family had been involved in shipowning and building since the early nineteenth century. Two members of the family moved to London in 1869 where they later established Turnbull, Scott & Co. Ltd.; they acquired their first steamer in 1882. The *Flowergate* was built in 1911 for German owners, but was allocated to Turnbull, Scott as a war prize in 1919, being bought by the firm in 1921. In this 1936 view she is seen under tow up 'the Drain' to the Roath Basin lock. This 5,166 gross ton steamer was broken up at Briton Ferry in 1946; the company that owned her ceased trading as shipowners in 1991.
(157/315)

**61.** The brothers John and Charles Harrison went into business as shipowners in London in 1888 with two second-hand steam colliers. By 1914, they had built up a fleet of eleven vessels, all of whose names began with the prefix 'Har-'. The *Harmonic* was a 4,558 gross ton steamer built at Sunderland in 1930 and is seen here approaching the Queen Alexandra lock, *c.* 1936. She was torpedoed and sunk in the south Atlantic on 5 May 1943. Harrisons ceased trading as shipowners in 1979.
(108/222)

**61**

**62**

**63**

**62.** The Bolton Steam Shipping Co. Ltd. was established by Frederic Bolton in London in 1884 and he took delivery of the newly-built steamer *Raphael* a year later. Most of the ships subsequently owned by the firm were named after artists. The *Rievaulx* was a 10,974 gross ton ore carrier built at Middlesbrough in 1958 and is seen here arriving at Cardiff with a cargo of iron ore for the East Moors steelworks, *c.* 1965. She was one of many vessels built for a specific fifteen-year BISCO (British Iron & Steel Company Ore) charter and was sold to Greek owners in 1973 upon the termination of that charter. The Bolton firm ceased shipowning in 1988.
(4271/21R)

**63.** The 3,918 gross ton steamer *Fylingdale* arriving at Cardiff, *c.* 1947. This vessel was built at Sunderland in 1924 and was owned by Headlam & Son of Whitby. The firm had its origins in the partnership of Rowland & Marwood, formed in 1886 and taken over by Headlam & Son in 1927. Until 1934 the company's funnel marking consisted of a red cross on a white band, but as this was an infringement of the international Red Cross emblem, the company had to change its mark to a blue cross that year. The *Fylingdale* was sold to Finnish owners in 1952.
(1143/1243)

**64.** One of 'Ropner's Navy'. Robert Ropner emigrated from his native Germany to West Hartlepool in 1858 and set up as a shipowner on his own account in 1874; by 1914 his company operated fifty-seven tramp steamers. The 5,207 gross ton *Haxby*, built at West Hartlepool in 1929, was typical of the 'long bridge deck' design of vessel operated by Ropners in the inter-war years. The *Haxby* was sunk by the German auxiliary cruiser *Orion* in the Atlantic on 24 April 1940.

**64**

**65.** The 4,795 gross ton steamer *Hermiston* was one of three sister vessels built between 1936 and 1939 for R. Chapman & Sons of Newcastle. All three vessels were built with the distinctive German-designed 'Maierform' bow, clearly visible in this view of the vessel arriving at Cardiff, *c.* 1948. Ralph Chapman first entered into shipowning holding shares in sailing vessels in the 1860s and the company that he later founded survived until 1974. The *Hermiston* was sold to Panamanian owners in 1960 and was wrecked on the Japanese coast in December 1967.
(2787/2812)

**66.** Captain Hugh Roberts was a native of Edern on the Llŷn Peninsula. He moved to Newcastle in 1874 and in 1877 established the North Shipping Co. Ltd. to acquire his first steamer, the *North Britain*. This photograph shows the *North Anglia* arriving at Cardiff, *c.* 1948. This 6,966 gross ton steamer was built at Sunderland in 1941 as the *Empire Wyclif* and was bought by North Shipping in 1946. Sold to Hong Kong owners in 1960, she was broken up at Hirohata, Japan in 1967. The North Shipping Co. Ltd. went out of existence in 1964 when it was taken over by another Newcastle firm, Common Brothers.
(2083/2146)

**67.** One of the most prominent of the once-numerous Newcastle-based shipping firms was the Moor Line which had its origins in 1885 when Captain Walter Runciman bought his first steamer. By 1914, Runciman was operating a fleet of forty modern steamers. Runciman was an early proponent of motor vessels, and the 4,972 gross ton *Fernmoor*, built in 1936, was an example of the Doxford 'Economy' motor tramp built in some numbers in the late 1930s. The *Fernmoor* was lost on 5 February 1954 when she ran aground off Palawan Island in the Philippines.
(370/668)

**65**

68

69

**68.** R. S. Dalgleish commenced business as a shipowner at Newcastle in 1906 with the purchase of a single second-hand steamer. Two further vessels were acquired by 1914. The *Pennyworth* was a 10,978 bulk ore carrier built for Dalgleish at Middlesbrough in 1958 and is seen here discharging a cargo of iron ore at the East Moors terminal in Cardiff's Roath Dock, *c.* 1970. She had been built for a specific fifteen-year BISCO (British Iron & Steel Company Ore) time charter and upon the termination of this charter she was sold to Greek owners in 1973. The Dalgleish firm went into voluntary liquidation in 1979.
(4195/9P)

**69.** The *Baron Haig* was one of the numerous vessels in the fleet of Hugh Hogarth & Sons of Ardossan. This well-known Scottish company was founded in the late 1860s, initially owning a number of sailing ships. The *Baron Haig* was a 3,391 gross ton steamer built at Irvine in 1926 and she served the company for over thirty years before her sale to Panamanian owners in January 1956. She was eventually stranded in the Black Sea in April 1963. This view was taken in the Queen Alexandra Dock, *c.* 1936.
(187/386)

**70.** The evening sun highlights the 5,824 gross ton steamer *Celtic Monarch* as she arrives at Cardiff, *c.* 1948. She was built at Port Glasgow in 1929 for Raeburn & Verel of Glasgow, a firm established in 1874. The *Celtic Monarch* was sold to owners in Hull in 1950. Raeburn & Verel ceased trading as shipowners with the sale of their last vessel in 1973.
(2195/2253)

70

**71.** A fine study of the *Cape Rodney* entering the Queen Alexandra lock at Cardiff, *c.* 1959, her deck cargo of sawn timber having caused her to develop a list to starboard. This 6,339 gross ton motor vessel was built at Glasgow in 1946 for the Lyle Shipping Co. Ltd. of Glasgow. This firm was established in 1903 by Alexander Park Lyle, son of the noted Greenock sugar merchant Abram Lyle whose company merged with Henry Tate & Sons of Liverpool in 1920 to form Tate & Lyle. The *Cape Rodney* was sold to Panamanian owners in 1963, whilst Lyle Shipping went into receivership in May 1987.
(3639/184C)

**72.** The 5,629 gross ton motor vessel *Lylepark*, built at Glasgow in 1951, photographed in the Queen Alexandra Dock, *c.* 1952. She was owned by the Denholm Line of Steamers Ltd., originally established at Greenock in 1866 by James Denholm, who was later joined by his brother John. The *Lylepark* was sold to Liberian interests in 1962, but Denholms are still in business today, owning two bulk carriers and managing a substantial fleet of vessels for owners world-wide.
(3107/3119)

**73.** The British Tanker Co. Ltd. was established in April 1915 as the original shipping division of the Anglo-Persian Oil Co. Ltd., re-named in 1954 as the British Petroleum Co. Ltd. (BP). The *British Harmony* was an 8,463 gross ton motor tanker built at Wallsend in 1941; she is seen here arriving at Cardiff, *c.* 1948. She continued in service until 1960 when she was sold and scrapped at Troon.
(1312/1411)

**71**

**74**

**75**

**74.** The *Flammulina* was an 8,203 gross ton motor tanker built at Belfast in 1943 as the *Empire Industry*. In 1946 she was bought by Anglo-Saxon Tankers, the shipping division of Shell Petroleum and re-named after a particular type of shell, as were all the Anglo-Saxon tankers. Seen here in the Roath Dock in the early 1950s, she was broken up at Hong Kong in 1960.
(3191/3193)

**75.** The *Esso Cardiff* was a motor tanker of 10,448 gross tons built at Portland, Oregon in 1945 to the standard American 'T2' design. In 1947 she was acquired by the Esso Transportation Co. Ltd., the shipping division of the Anglo-American Oil Co. Ltd., and given the name *Esso Cardiff*. She was sold to Liberian owners in 1954 and was later converted into an oil/ore carrier. Having suffered severe damage on a trans-Atlantic passage, she was broken up at Castellon in 1965. A second *Esso Cardiff* was built in 1963 and broken up in Korea in 1983.
(3097/3109)

**76.** The company of Charles Hill & Sons of Bristol has been associated with shipping and shipbuilding in the city since the eighteenth century. In 1879 they established the Bristol City Line, operating a regular service from Bristol Channel ports to New York. One of the older vessels owned by the firm during the post-war period was the *New York City*, a 2,736 gross ton steamer built at Hill's own Bristol shipyard in 1917. This view was taken on 23 March 1947, some three years prior to her sale to Turkish owners in 1950.
(1459/1554)

**77**

**78**

FORTH BANK

**77.** Belfast's best-known shipping firm was the Head Line, founded in 1877 by James and Frederick Heyn, sons of Gustavus Heyn, the former Prussian consul in Belfast. Head Line operated a cargo liner service from Belfast to numerous ports on the eastern seaboard of north America, with feeder services from certain European ports, particularly in the Baltic. The *Bengore Head* was a 2,609 gross ton steamer built at West Hartlepool in 1922, and is seen here discharging pit wood at Cardiff, *c.* 1936. She was torpedoed and sunk in the north Atlantic on 9 May 1941.
(257/471)

**78.** Andrew Weir established himself as a shipowner at Glasgow in 1885. He acquired his first steamer in 1896 and by the 1920s an extensive world-wide network of cargo liner routes had been established under the title of the Bank Line Ltd. The *Forthbank*, seen here arriving at Cardiff, *c.* 1950, was a 5,057 gross ton steamer built at Belfast in 1929. Sold to Italian owners in 1953, she was broken up in Hong Kong in 1959.
(3006/3023)

**79.** Known in Cardiff as the 'Grange boats', the vessels of the Houlder Line were regular visitors to the port, carrying cargoes of refrigerated meat from South America. The distinctive outline of these vessels can be seen clearly in this view of the *Hornby Grange* in the Queen Alexandra Dock, *c.* 1950. She was a refrigerated motor vessel of 10,785 gross tons, built at Newcastle in 1946. By this date, Houlder Line was part of the Furness Withy group.
(3010/3026)

**80.** Clan Line was established in 1878 when Charles Cayzer acquired two steamers to operate a service to Bombay. The firm later extended its operations to other parts of India and South Africa. *Clan Brodie* was built at Greenock in 1940, and was originally the seaplane depot ship HMS *Athene*. She was bought by Clan Line in 1946 and converted into a conventional cargo vessel of 7,473 gross tons. Seen here in the Queen Alexandra Dock, *c.* 1952, she was eventually broken up at Hong Kong in 1963.
(3240/3228)

**81.** Blue Star Line was founded by the brothers William and Edmund Vestey in 1912. The brothers also owned the Dewhurst retail butchery chain and Blue Star vessels have always been associated with the carriage of refrigerated meat from South America and later from Australia and New Zealand. *Newcastle Star* was a motor vessel of 8,398 gross tons, built in West Germany in 1956; she is seen here alongside the Cold Stores in the Queen Alexandra Dock, *c.* 1970. Sold to Cypriot owners in 1975, she was broken up in Taiwan in 1980.
(4141/9N)

**82.** Since 1956 the port of Barry has been associated with the Geest Line and its service to the Windward Islands. This service was operated with chartered tonnage for some years before the decision was taken to acquire tonnage in 1964. The *Geestcape* was a 7,679 gross ton refrigerated motor vessel, built at Greenock in 1966 and seen here in the No. 2 Dock at Barry, *c.* 1972. She was sold to French owners in 1975. Geest's association with Barry was sadly terminated early in 1993.
(3812/6G)

80

# ~ 4 ~

# *Tugs, Trawlers and Dredgers*

**83.** The 181 gross ton steam tug *Cardiff Rose* in the West Bute Dock, *c.* 1959. Built at South Shields in 1914 as *Lady Duncannon* for the Dover Harbour Board, she came to Cardiff in 1958 when she was purchased by I. C. Guy & Co. of Cardiff. This firm went into voluntary liquidation in 1963 when most of its local interests were taken over by R. & J. H. Rea of London.
(3584/68C)

**84**

**85**

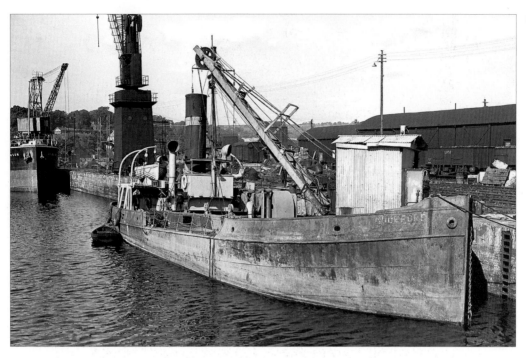

**84.** The steam tug *Caroline Davies* moves away from the Federal Line motor vessel *Cumberland* in the Queen Alexandra Dock on 12 April 1958. Built at Dumbarton in 1907 for a Montreal towage firm, this 197 gross ton tug later saw service on the Manchester Ship Canal before she was bought by J. Davies Towage and Salvage Co., Cardiff, in 1952. Note that the starboard anchor cable is paid out; the anchor is hanging just below the keel of the vessel, ready to let go should the need arise, but low enough to avoid damage to the hull should the tug come up against the quay wall.
(3071/3083)

**85.** Cardiff's only trawling company, Neale & West, was founded as a fish merchants' business in 1885. Their first trawler was acquired in 1888 and the firm later adopted a series of distinctive Japanese names for their vessels. In this view the 340 gross ton *Muroto*, built at Stockton-on-Tees in 1931, is seen hurrying home to the firm's base at the bottom of the West Bute Dock, *c.* 1948. Neale & West ceased trading in 1956.
(1025/1126)

**86.** The little grab dredger *Mudeford* (invariably pronounced 'Muddyford' by those who remember her!) at Penarth Dock, *c.* 1951. Built for the Great Western Railway at Zaltbommel in the Netherlands in 1924, the 232 gross ton vessel was used mainly within the dock complex at Cardiff, dredging along the quay walls. She would also make the occasional foray up the Taff to dredge at the pumping station for the timber pond below Penarth Road bridge; this involved opening the Clarence Road swingbridge, and the *Mudeford* was probably the last vessel for which this was done.
(3160/3166)

**87.** The dredging of aggregates for the building industry from the sea-bed of the Bristol Channel dates back to 1912. One of the largest vessels used in this trade was the aptly-named 3,145 gross ton *Sand Galore*, originally built at Birkenhead in 1935 as the Mersey mud-dredger *Hoyle*. When this photograph was taken (*c.* 1964), she was owned by the London-based Sand & Gravel Marketing Co. Ltd. Note the long suction pipe amid-ships which was lowered to the sea-bed to obtain her cargo of sand and gravel. (4317/10S)

# ~ 5 ~

# *Under Sail*

**88.** A typical Welsh schooner, the 118 gross ton *Camborne* was built at Amlwch in 1884 for local owners. In 1920 she was acquired by the Hook Colliery Co. Ltd., near Haverfordwest, to carry anthracite from their jetty on the Cleddau to France. Her rigging was reduced and a diesel engine installed, but she was not a success. She was then sold to Captain Hugh Shaw of Arlingham, Glos., who managed to trade her successfully around the British coasts for many years thereafter.
(552/H824)

89

90

**89.** The 98 gross ton wooden ketch *Irene* was built at Bridgwater in 1907 and was often employed in the carriage of bricks and earthenware products from the Somerset port. She continued to trade until 1960. Extensively re-built in the 1980s, her home port is now Bristol, from which she regularly undertakes charter work. She is seen here in the West Bute Dock, *c.* 1936.
(789/H1066)

**90.** Amongst the last sailing vessels to trade regularly to Cardiff were the beautiful Breton schooners that imported pit wood and vegetables from Brittany and the Bay of Biscay. It was also on these vessels that the 'Shoni Winiwns' – the Breton onion sellers – travelled to Wales. The schooners returned to Brittany with cargoes of coal, as in this view of the 102 gross ton *Françoise* under tow, outward bound, *c.* 1936. She is setting her mainsail, whilst on her foremast can be seen the roller-reefing square topsail so typical of these Breton schooners.
**(479)**

**91.** Many of the Breton schooners were built originally for service in the great cod-fishing fleet that left Brittany every spring to fish off southern Iceland. The 182 gross ton *Glycine* was built at Paimpol in 1911 as a 'chasseur', a fast sailing vessel that took salt up to the fishing fleet, returning with the best of the new season's cod. By the late 1930s, however, she had been relegated to the pit-wood trade and is seen here arriving at Cardiff with such a cargo. Note the discharging gaff with its block and tackle already rigged on the foremast.
**(476)**

**92.** The last European shipowner to operate deep-sea sailing vessels was Gustav Erikson of the Åland Islands in the Baltic. One of numerous such vessels that he bought in the 1920s was the 3,111 gross ton barque *Herzogin Cecilie*, built originally as a sail-training vessel in 1902. Erikson employed these vessels in the grain trade from Australia, and this view was taken when the vessel discharged grain from Port Lincoln at Cardiff in April 1928.
(828)

**93.** Another vessel in the Erikson fleet originally built as a sail-training vessel was the 2,670 gross ton barque *Viking*. Built in 1906 for the Danish Schoolship Association, she was bought by Erikson in 1929 and is seen here off Cardiff with a cargo of grain from Australia in June 1939. She survives as a schoolship at Göteborg, Sweden.
(485)

**94.** The 3,091 gross ton barque *Passat* was built in Hamburg in 1911 for F. Laeisz's 'Flying "P" Line' of nitrate traders. Together with her elder sister *Pamir* she was sold to Gustav Erikson in 1932, and in 1949 they were the last sailing ships to carry grain from Australia, the *Passat* discharging 56,000 bags of wheat at Barry before joining *Pamir* at Penarth in October that year. They lay there until 1951. The *Pamir* was lost at sea in 1957 whilst in service as a German sail-training vessel, but the *Passat* survives at Travemunde in Germany.
(3343)

**95.** The high freight rates prevailing during the First World War and the years immediately following led to a remarkable revival in wooden shipbuilding in the USA and Canada. Most of the vessels built were substantial schooners, and the last of them was the five-masted 1,512 gross ton *Edna Hoyt*, built at Thomaston, Maine in 1920. Seen here approaching Cardiff under tow *c.* 1936, she continued to trade until condemned at Lisbon in 1937.
(337/622)

94

95

# ~ 6 ~

# Navies of the World

**96.** The Royal Yacht *Britannia* arriving at Cardiff in the summer of 1969, bringing Prince Charles to Wales in the year of his investiture. This 3,990 ton vessel was built on the Clyde in 1953 and is the most recent in a long line of royal yachts dating back to the reign of Charles II. The *Britannia* was decommissioned in 1997 and is currently a tourist attraction at the port of Leith.
(3317)

**97**

**98**

**97.** The 9,550 ton cruiser HMS *Tiger* entering the Queen Alexandra Dock in October 1966. Laid down on the Clyde in 1941 as HMS *Bellerophon*, she was not completed until 1959. During this particular visit to Cardiff, her crew were called upon to assist in rescue work at the Aberfan disaster. This was also the vessel on board which discussions took place between Harold Wilson and Ian Smith following the latter's declaration of independence for Rhodesia in 1965. Having been laid up at Plymouth for some years, this vessel was broken up at Castellon, Spain, in 1986.
(4451/23T)

**98.** The 5,600 ton guided-missile destroyer HMS *Glamorgan* at Cardiff, *c.* 1974. This vessel was built on the Tyne in 1964 and was one of the County class of guided-missile destroyers. Note the awnings and side-screens on the foredeck, presumably for a civic reception. This vessel was sold to the Chilean Navy in 1986 and re-named *Almirante Latorre*.
(3831/18G)

**99.** The 2,170 ton frigate HMS *Llandaff* entering the Queen Alexandra Dock, *c.* 1972. Built on the Clyde in 1955, she was a vessel in the Salisbury class of frigates, all named after British cathedral cities. She was sold to the Bangladesh Navy in 1976 and re-named *Domar Farooq*.
(4049/24L)

**100.** The minesweeper HMS *St David* arriving at Cardiff, *c.* 1965. This 360 ton Ton class minesweeper was built as the *Crichton* but bore the name *St David* from 1961 until 1976 during the period that she was allocated to the south Wales division of the Royal Naval Reserve, HMS Cambria.
(4386/55S)

**101.** The Castle class corvettes were built to serve as convoy escorts during the Second World War. Built on the Clyde in 1944, HMS *Allington Castle* is seen here in the Roath Basin in 1947. Note the early lantern-type radar at the masthead. She was broken up at Sunderland in 1958.
(922/1028)

**102.** The submarine depot ship HMS *Forth* was, at 8,900 tons, one of the largest vessels in the Royal Navy, aircraft carriers excepted. Built at Glasgow in 1938, she was moored on the Clyde for most of the Second World War, acting as a depot ship for submarines operating in the north Atlantic. For this purpose she carried a wide range of facilities such as a foundry, machine shops, torpedo repair shops and plant for charging submarines' batteries. She was sold in 1985 and broken up at Kingsnorth.
(3784/20F)

103

104

**103.** The 440 ton H-class submarine *H34* approaching the East Bute Basin, *c.* 1937. Built at Birkenhead in 1918, she was sold by the Royal Navy after the Second World War, and broken up at Troon late in 1945. (495)

**104.** By way of direct contrast with the previous picture is this view of the nuclear-powered submarine *Churchill* in the Queen Alexandra lock *c.* 1973. Built at Barrow in 1968, she was one of the Valiant class of Fleet submarines. She has recently been withdrawn from service with the Royal Navy. (3579/64C)

**105.** The Dutch frigate *Amsterdam* in the Roath Basin, *c.* 1972. Built in the city after which she was named in 1958, this vessel was one of the Friesland class of frigates, all of which were named after provinces and cities in the Netherlands. The entire class has gradually been withdrawn since 1975. (3454/66A)

**106.** The French Navy's patrol vessel *L'Attentif* pictured in the Roath Basin, *c.* 1972. This 325 ton diesel-powered vessel was launched at Lorient on 5 October 1957.
(3910/43H)

**107.** The 2,400 ton Gearing class destroyer USS *Cone* approaching the entrance lock to Newport Docks, *c.* 1947. She was built in 1945 at Bethlehem, Staten Island, New York.
(958/1062)

**108.** This unidentified Canadian submarine is one of three sister vessels of the Oberon class built for the Canadian Navy at Chatham in 1962–4. The three 2,200 ton sisters were all named after Canadian Indian tribes. The protuberance above the bow carries the vessel's sonar equipment.
(4395/62S)

# ~ 7 ~

# *From Oceans' Farthest Coasts*

**109.** Irish Shipping Ltd. was established in 1941 with the intention of building up a merchant fleet to supply Eire during the Second World War. By 1943, fifteen somewhat aged vessels had been acquired, one of which was the 3,192 gross ton *Irish Larch*. Acquired from Palestinian owners in 1941, she had been built in 1903 as *Tregothnan* for Hain of St Ives. Sold to Turkish owners in 1949, she was finally broken up at Trieste in 1961.
(946/1052)

**110**

**111**

**110.** The 3,908 gross ton *Garryvale* was one of the numerous turret-deck steamers built by William Doxford & Sons of Sunderland between 1892 and 1911. This peculiar design imparted a number of advantages such as increased longitudinal strength and greater deadweight capacity in relation to net tonnage. Built in 1907 for A. Crawford, Barr & Co. of Glasgow, she was owned by Kristian Hansen of Helsingfors, Finland, when this photograph was taken, *c*. 1936.
(733/H1004)

**111.** The *Oscar Gorthon* was a steamer of 1,814 gross tons built at Fredrikstad, Norway, in 1939 for the Gorthon Shipping firm of Helsingborg in Sweden. She was built to the 'boilers on deck' design adopted by many Scandinavian shipowners in which the boilers were placed above the engines at main deck level to maximize cargo space. She was broken-up in Greece in 1971, and the company which she served was merged with another Swedish shipping company in 2005.
(1792/1876)

**112.** One of the best-known German shipping firms was the Hamburg-Amerika Linie, established in 1847 with four small sailing vessels. In this 1936 view the 5,062 gross ton *Frankenwald*, built at Hamburg in 1922 is assisted into the Queen Alexandra lock by the local tug *Margaret Ham*. Originally built for the company's Hamburg to West Coast South America service, she had accomodation for ten first-class passengers. She was wrecked forty miles north of Bergen whilst bound from Narvik to Germany with iron ore on 6 January 1940. Note the Swastika ensign of the Third Reich flying on the poop.
(680/H951)

**113.** The Maersk Line, established in 1904, was owned by A. P. Moller of Copenhagen; apart from general tramping, the firm also had a regular service from the Far East to Los Angeles and New York. The *Emilie Maersk* was one of their smaller tramps (2,202 gross tons) and is seen here in the Queen Alexandra Dock, *c.* 1936. Today, Maersk is one of the world's leading container ship operators, managing a massive fleet of over five hundred vessels.
(672/H941)

**114.** The distinctive 'JL' funnel mark on this vessel betray its owners as J. Lauritzen of Copenhagen. The *Chilean Reefer*, built in 1936, was one of a number of refrigerated motor vessels built for Lauritzen in the late 1930s to carry fruit from the Mediterranean and West Africa to northern European ports. This view of the 4,360 gross ton vessel was taken at Cardiff, *c.* 1937.
(562/H834)

**115.** The world's first successful ocean-going motor vessel was the *Selandia*, built in 1912 by Burmeister & Wain of Copenhagen for the well-known Danish East-Asiatic Line. The 6,956 gross ton *Chile* seen here was a later sister vessel built by the same firm in 1915. These vessels had a particularly distinctive outline, in that they had no funnels; gases from the engine were exhausted through pipes incorporated in the mizzen mast (third from the bow).
(566/H836)

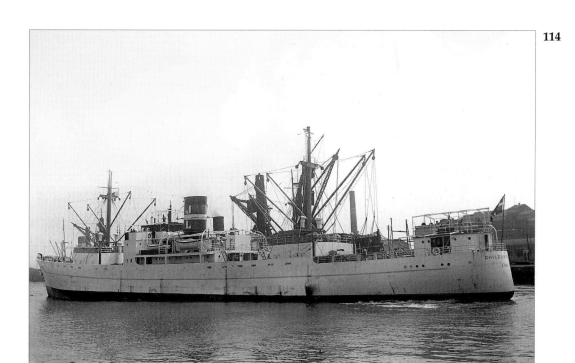

**116**

**117**

**116.** The notion that land-locked Switzerland has a merchant fleet may sound strange to some, but the Swiss flag flying at the poop of the 6,316 gross ton *Silvaplana* proves that such a fleet exists! This 1956-built ship was owned by the Suisse Atlantique Soc. de Armaments Maritime of Basle and registered at that Swiss city.
(4350/29S)

**117.** The 306 gross ton Dutch coaster *Fivel* approaching the Roath Basin lock with a deck cargo of sawn timber, *c.* 1937. Built at Groningen in 1936, she was typical of the small and efficient motor coasters developed during the 1930s by Dutch builders. Requiring a smaller crew as there were no firemen, and carrying oil bunkers in their double bottoms, vessels such as these posed a serious threat to the traditional steam coaster still favoured by many British owners at the time.
(694/H964)

**118.** Four swans add a graceful touch to this view of the Estonian steamer *Arcturus* as she discharges her cargo of pit wood, *c.* 1936. This 1,682 gross ton steamer was built on the Tyne in 1890 and was owned by J. Rang of Tallinn at the time this photograph was taken.
(398/706)

**118**

**119.** A century ago, nobody would have dreamed that one day coal would be imported to Cardiff! But in 1972, the 12,705 gross ton bulk carrier *Robert L. D.* was pictured arriving at Cardiff with a cargo of American coal for the Central Electricity Generating Board, coal that would then be blended with south Wales steam coal for use in local power stations. This vessel was owned by the well-known Parisian shipping firm Louis Dreyfus & Cie. and was part of the Gearbulk pool of vessels in which British, French and Norwegian shipping firms participated. Note the gantry cranes and the discharging grabs on deck. (4292/35R)

**120.** Greek-owned tramp steamers were a familiar sight in Cardiff, many of them having been built originally for Cardiff owners. An exception was the 4,816 gross ton *Eugenie Livanos* built in 1936 by Gray of West Hartlepool for Livanos Bros. of Piraeus. She was one of eight similar vessels built new for this firm in British yards in 1936–8. (649/H916)

**121.** The 5,200 gross ton *Anna*, owned by N. D. Lykiardopulo of Athens, in the Queen Alexandra Dock, *c*. 1947. Note the wartime life-rafts suspended in the rigging of the masts. This vessel was built at Greenock in 1919 as *Leapark* for J. & J. Denholm of Glasgow. (1041/1142)

119

122

КОРСУНЬ-ШЕВЧЕНКОВСКИЙ

123

WILLIAM H. JACKSON

**122.** One of the vessels that made up the massive merchant fleet of the former USSR was the 1925 gross ton steamer *Korsun Shevchenkovskiy*, seen here arriving at Cardiff with a cargo of sawn timber, *c.* 1970. This vessel was built at Lekkerkerk in the Netherlands in 1943 for the Hamburg–Amerika Linie. Seized as a war prize in May 1945, she was allocated to the Soviet Union in 1946 and remained in service with the USSR's Baltic fleet until she was cut up at Ghent early in 1972.
(3567/50C)

**123.** The ship that won the war; one of the 2,710 Liberty ships built in the USA between 1941 and 1945 to replace Allied shipping losses. Built at the Bethlehem–Fairfield shipyard, Baltimore, in 1943, the *William H. Jackson* was sold to Greek owners in 1947 and eventually cut up at Shanghai in December 1968. These 7,176 gross ton vessels were built to a design based upon the Sunderland-built steamer *Dorington Court* of 1939.
(930/1035)

**124.** Whereas the Liberty ship was the standard American tramp-type vessel of the Second World War, the Victory ship was its cargo liner equivalent. The *Lawrence Victory* was built at Portland, Oregon, in 1945; these vessels had a standard gross tonnage of 7,607 and had steam turbine engines capable of driving the ship at 16 knots. When this view was taken at Cardiff in 1948, the *Lawrence Victory* was a unit of the US Army transport fleet.
(2028/2095)

**125.** The 8,228 gross ton *American Producer* was an example of another standard American type, the 'C2'. Built at Oakland, California in 1943, she was owned by the prominent American shipping firm, United States Lines of New York, that also owned the crack American passenger liners *America* and *United States*. She is seen here arriving at Cardiff in the late 1950s.
(3381/16A)

**126.** The *Arosa*, seen here in the Roath Dock, *c.* 1948, was built at Three Rivers near Quebec in 1922 for service on the Great Lakes. She is easily identified as a Great Lakes vessel by her bridge located right forward on the forecastle. Many of these vessels found themselves in trans-Atlantic convoys during the Second World War, and by the date of this photograph she was owned by Panamanian shipowners, operating far away from the waters for which she was originally built.
(1409/1509)

**127.** The 5,102 gross ton *Jalausha* was owned by the Bombay-based Scindia Steam Navigation Co. Ltd., having been built by her owners at their Vizagapatam yard in 1948. Established in 1919, the company ran a regular cargo service from various Indian ports to Europe. This view was taken as the vessel approached the Roath Basin lock, *c.* 1949.
(2370/2421)

**128.** Hong Kong was the home of a number of well-known shipping firms, such as John Manners & Co. Ltd., owners of the *Sydney Breeze*. This 5,386 gross ton vessel was originally built at Sunderland in 1949 as *Trelevan* for the Hain Steamship Co. Ltd., and was sold to Manners in 1964. She was eventually broken up in Spain in 1974.
(4409/71S)

# Bibliography

For further details on the ships pictured in this book, readers are referred to the following publications:

## 1. Works of Reference

*British Vessels Lost at Sea, 1939–1945*, (1947)
*Janes's Fighting Ships*, (various dates)
*Lloyd's Register*, (various dates)
*Mercantile Navy List*, (various dates)

## 2. Printed Books

Appleyard, Harold, *Turnbull Scott*, (1978)
— *Bank Line*, (1985)
Atkinson, Tony and Kevin O'Donoghue, *Blue Star*, (1985)
Axelson, Kjell and Tomas Joahanesson, *The Gorthon Shipping Companies, 1915–1985*, (1985)
Colledge, J. J., *Ships of the Royal Navy*, (2nd edn, 1987)
Dunn, Laurence, *Ship Recognition – Merchant Ships*, (n.d.)
Fenton, Roy, *Monks's Navy*, (1981)
— *Cambrian Coasters*, (1989)
Gibbs, John Morel, *Morels of Cardiff*, (1982)
Gray, Leonard, *The Ropner Fleet*, 1874–1974, (1975)
Greenhill, Basil, *The Merchant Schooners*, (2nd ed., 1988)
— and Hackman, John, *The Grain Races*, (1986)
Harvey, W. J., *Head Line*, (1990)
Heaton, Paul M., *The Redbrook; a deep sea tramp*, (1981)
— *The Usk Ships*, (1982)
— *The Abbey Line*, (1983)
— *Reardon Smith Line*, (1984)
— *The South American Saint Line*, (1985)
— *Tatems of Cardiff*, (1987)
— *Jack Billmeir: Merchant Shipowner*, (1989)
— *Welsh Shipping; Forgotten Fleets*, (1989)
Hill, J. C. G., *Shipshape and Bristol Fashion*, (1951)
Hope, Iain, *The Campbells of Kilmun*, (1981)
Jenkins, J. Geraint, *Evan Thomas, Radcliffe*, (1982)
Langmuir, G. E. and G. H. Somner, *William Sloan & Co. Ltd., Glasgow, 1825–1968*, (1987)
Lingwood, John and Harold Appleyard, *Chapman of Newcastle*, (1985)

MacRae, J. A. and C. V. Waine, *The Steam Collier Fleets*, (1990)

Middlemiss, N. L., *Gathering of the Clans*, (1988)

— *Travels of the Tramps*, (Vols. 1 & 2, 1989 & 1991)

— *The British Tankers*, (1990)

— *The Anglo Saxon/Shell Tankers*, (1990)

Mitchell, W. H. and L. A. Sawyer, *The Liberty Ships*, (2nd ed., 1985)

— *Sailing Ship to Supertanker*, (1987)

— *The Empire Ships*, (2nd ed., 1990)

O'Donoghue, Kevin and Harold Appleyard, *Hain of St Ives*, (1986)

Spong, H. C., *Irish Shipping Ltd.*, (1982)

Talbot-Booth, E. C., *Merchant Shipping*, (1942)

Thomas, P. N., *British Steam Tugs*, (1983)

Underhill, H. A., *Sail Training and Cadet Ships*, (1956)

Waine, C. V., *Steam Coasters and Short-Sea Traders*, (1977)

Williams, Desmond I., *Seventy Years in Shipping*, (1989)

## 3. Articles

Cressey, Roy, 'Holderness Steamship Co. Ltd.', *Ships Monthly*, January–March, 1988.

Gosson, P. R. and R. M. Parsons, 'The Golden Cargo', *Ships Monthly*, June, July, 1987.

Heaton, Paul M., 'Gibbs of Newport', *Sea Breezes*, November, 1978.

— 'A Celtic Venture', *Sea Breezes*, July, 1979.

— 'Under Two Flags – the Geest Line Story', *Sea Breezes*, May 1981.

— 'A Brave Post-War Venture', *Sea Breezes*, June 1981.

— 'Graig Shipping: A Firm Foundation', *Sea Breezes*, August, September, 1982.

Parsons, R. M., 'Mighty Miniatures of the Bristol Coal Trade', *Sea Breezes*, January 1993.

# Index of Ships' Names

References are given in the form of page numbers.